EVER
GO

BANANAS?

EVOTIONS FOR KIDS

WILLIAM
COLEMAN

Chariot Books™
David C. Cook Publishing Co.

Chariot Books™ is an imprint of Chariot Family Publishing
Cook Communications Ministries, Elgin, Illinois 60120
Cook Communications Ministries, Paris, Ontario
Kingsway Communications, Eastbourne, England

DO YOU EVER GO BANANAS
©1993 by William Coleman

Illustrations and design by Helen Lannis
First Printing, 1993
Printed in the United States of America
97 96 95 94   5 4 3

Library of Congress Cataloging-in-Publication Data
Coleman, William L.
Do you ever go bananas?: devotions for kids/William Coleman.
p. cm.
Summary: A collection of devotional readings, including "Sneering at Jesus," "Reason to Cheer Up," and "Losing a
Friend."
ISBN: 1-55513-738-5
1. Children—Prayer—books and devotions—English. [1. Prayer books and devotions]   I. Title
BV4870.C63144   1992
242'.62—dc20

                                                                                    92-627
                                                                                    CIP
                                                                                    AC

Table of Contents

Sneering from the Inside

If we are upset at someone and we want to show him, we often make faces. Maybe we squeeze our lips tightly together to look irritated. Some of us lower our foreheads down over our eyes to look especially upset. Others of us are nose wrinklers.

A group of religious leaders, called Pharisees, were listening to Jesus speak. They got upset at what He said. This wasn't unusual. The Pharisees disliked many of the things that Jesus said.

One time, Jesus told the crowd they couldn't love both God and money. No one can have two masters, because we serve one or the other, He explained.

That statement may not sound too surprising to you, but the Pharisees were furious. They loved money. Who was Jesus, they figured, to tell them they couldn't love both God and money? The Bible says the Pharisees began to sneer at Jesus.

Sneering means they gave Jesus their ugliest mean looks. They stared hard at the Son of God and tried to scare Him. Maybe some turned red in the face to show how mad they were. One Pharisee probably puffed up his cheeks like he was steaming. Another may have bit his tongue because he was so aggravated.

Their nastiest sneers didn't frighten Jesus. He knew they loved money more than they loved God and He had known they would get upset. Sneering is dumb. It doesn't solve any problems. Sneering doesn't help us deal with what is really bothering us.

JESUS TOLD THE CROWD THEY COULDN'T LOVE BOTH GOD AND MONEY.

5

THE LOVE OF GOD IS MORE VALUABLE THAN ALL THE RICHES IN THE WORLD.

Instead of making faces at Jesus, the Pharisee would have been smarter to give up their love for money. The love of God is more valuable than all the riches in the world. (Luke 16:13-15)

MAKING FACES

Twist your face the same way your brother or sister does when he or she is angry. Twist your face the same way your parent does when he or she is upset. Twist your face the same way you do when you get upset.

PICK AND CHOOSE

When you say or do something wrong, would you rather have your parent:

a. sneer at you?

   or

b. tell you what is wrong?

   Why?

   Do you communicate with your brother and sister by making faces or by using words? Explain.

SNEERING COMES FROM INSIDE

People who feel good inside don't need to make nasty faces. If we follow Jesus, we won't need to be upset so often. It is almost always better to say what we mean than to make ugly faces.

SCRIPTURE READING: Luke 16:14

PRAYER STARTER: *"Dear God, help my face show love instead of sneering."*

The Three Teachers

When Suzanne started having many teachers, she felt like a real student. In one class she studied history, in another class English and in another math. An hour with each teacher seemed like plenty of time to spend in one place.

Having different teachers also gave Suzanne a chance to see how each teacher had his or her own approach to learning.

Mrs. Novak was the meanest. When she gave a math test she acted like she wanted everyone to do poorly. A middle-aged teacher, Mrs. Novak didn't explain much and tried to fool the students with surprise questions. Most of the students got low grades and hated the class.

Suzanne could see a sharp contrast in her next class. Mr. Tuttle, a nice, even-tempered man, didn't appear to get too involved. He did his job and went home. How the students did on history tests was of little concern to him. Mr. Tuttle explained the material, gave the test, and didn't get too excited.

The teacher who stood out the most for Suzanne was Miss Bergman. She wanted everyone to do well on her English tests and it showed. She never made the test easy, but Miss Bergman took a personal interest in her students and tried to prepare them well. She never tried to trick anyone. She didn't feel good when a student failed.

Each teacher did the job, but Miss Bergman worked hard to make sure everyone was prepared.

GOD WANTS EVERYONE TO PASS HIS TESTS.

God also gives tests because challenges help develop into better people. But God isn't like the first two teachers. He is interested in helping us every way he can. God wants everyone to pass.

HOW MIGHT GOD TEST US?

Which one might God allow?
1. Flatten our bike tires?
2. Give us head lice?
3. Lock us in an ice-cream factory?
4. Help us meet a lonely friend?
5. Introduce us to a hungry family?

ANGRY WITH GOD

Have you ever been angry with God because you asked Him for something and didn't get it? Do you think waiting was part of the test? How did you do?

EYE TEST

An optometrist or an ophthalmologist usually tests our eyes. They don't test us in order to pass or flunk us. Their goal is to help us see the best we can.

If we need corrective lenses like contacts or glasses, the doctor tries to improve our vision. Any test given to make us better is a good experience.

SCRIPTURE READING: Genesis 22:1

PRAYER STARTER: *"God, keep me alert so can pass the good tests You send my way."*

8

Heidi Had an Attitude

Every time the ski instructor spoke, Heidi seemed to huff. "If you keep your knees bent, you will have better control of your skis and you can keep your balance better. Like this."

As the instructor demonstrated the moves, Heidi twisted to each side without concentrating.

"When you fall down, first pull your skis free from the snow and then use your poles to pull back up on your feet," he explained. *Big deal,* Heidi thought. "Boring, boring," she whispered.

Heidi hated to listen to directions. She thought she knew more than most people. No one could tell her what to do. Heidi had an attitude that hung over her head like a dark cloud. She griped and complained most of the time.

HEIDI HAD AN ATTITUDE THAT HUNG OVER HER HEAD LIKE A DARK CLOUD.

"One at a time," the instructor announced. "Give everyone plenty of room. Don't be afraid. Just keep your knees bent."

Steadily each student took a turn pushing off from the top of the slope. Some fell down only a few yards from the starting point. Others skied a zigzag, unable to keep a straight path.

The sixth person down the hill was Heidi. Standing tall and rigid, poles shaking in her hands, screaming at the top of her lungs, she raced down the hill totally out of control.

Swishing toward a wide bush, Heidi crossed her arms over her eyes. Head first she tumbled into the bush and sprawled across its top. Skis and poles spread in every direction.

9

Bewildered, Heidi shook her head and said, "Why don't they teach you how to use these stupid skis before they send you out?"

THE HEIDI LOOK-ALIKE

1. Have you ever had an attitude like Heidi's?
2. Do you hate to listen to instructions?
3. Sometimes are you hard to get along with?
4. Do you ever feel like a know-it-all?
5. If your friends described your general attitude, what might they say?

ATTITUDE ADJUSTMENT

How to improve your attitude:

1. Try to be kinder to everyone.
2. Treat others as you would like to be treated.
3. Ask how Jesus Christ would act in this situation.
4. Allow God to make you more thoughtful of others.
5. Never be too proud to learn from others.

INSTANT ATTITUDE

If a parent asks you to straighten up your room, your first reaction is:

to say okay
to blame your brother
to stomp off
to get right to it
to pout

SCRIPTURE READING: Ephesians 4:22-24

PRAYER STARTER: *"Lord, help me change my attitude."*

10

Reason to Cheer Up

"Hey, Hey! Over here!" The blind man shouted. "I could use a little help myself!" "S-h-h-h! Keep him quiet, somebody. Put a muzzle on that guy." People in the crowd tried to shut up the poor beggar.

"Jesus, Son of David, be kind to me!" he yelled, despite everyone's efforts to stifle him.

The scene was getting tense. One persistent man kept calling out for some attention while those standing around were embarrassed to have him there. They didn't want this disabled street person bugging the Son of God.

Suddenly a voice cut across the noise telling the crowd to bring the blind beggar closer. They could barely believe their ears. Jesus told them to lead the blind man through the crowd.

In a second, their attitudes changed. Instead of telling him to shut up they began saying, "Cheer up, cheer up." The same person they had told to get lost they now told to get up and start moving toward Christ.

Everyone's attitude changed immediately. The crowd was excited and treated him like a special guest. The man tossed his cloak aside and bounced to his feet. Jesus Christ had accepted him, and the blind man knew that the Son of God could give him new life.

From gloom and unhappiness the blind man found reason to be cheerful and excited. In that moment, Jesus also gave him his sight back (Mark 10:46-52).

THEY DIDN'T WANT THIS DISABLED STREET PERSON BUGGING THE SON OF GOD.

11

WHAT TIME OF DAY ARE YOU MOST CHEERFUL?

1. Breakfast?
2. Lunchtime?
3. Supper time?
4. Evenings?
5. Bedtime?

WHAT IS THE BEST WAY TO CHEER YOU UP?

1. Tickle you?
2. Fix nachos?
3. Give you money?
4. Go skateboarding?
5. Go to the dentist?

When you think about Jesus, how does He help make you feel cheerful? What does He mean to you?

The Dictionary Says Cheerfulness Is "To be glad or happy; to have hope or courage; to get rid of gloom or worry"

PLUMS AND PRUNES

The next time you feel dumpy and your face shrivels up like a prune, you might talk to Christ about it. Try asking Him to remind you of things you should be happy about. You could also ask Him to show you ways to cheer others up.

SCRIPTURE READING: Proverbs 12:25

PRAYER STARTER: *"When my face is sagging and my heart is dragging, help me think of You, Christ, and bring cheer to my life."*

The Crooked Paperboy

"Thank you, Mrs. Hovel." Matt shoved the change into his pocket and hurried off to the next apartment.

"Paper, Mr. Saylor," Matt smiled as he handed a newspaper to the elderly gentleman. "Oh, thanks for the tip."

Every day Matt delivered newspapers to four neighbors in his apartment house. Two of the neighbors paid Matt daily and the other two paid at the end of each week. Each customer gave him a small tip. This service had gone on for several weeks and seemed to serve everyone well.

Even Matt's parents were happy. He volunteered to go daily and pick up a paper for them. Matt took a quarter from the desk at home and walked two blocks to the newspaper machine. He would slide his quarter through the slot, open the door and remove five newspapers. He then returned to his apartment house and delivered the stolen papers.

Some days Matt felt bad about his crooked scheme; but when his conscience began to bother him, Matt would convince himself that it was all right. After all, he argued, the newspaper company has plenty of papers. They probably didn't even know how many papers they lose each day. If a twelve-year-old boy makes a dollar or so, who really cares?

As the days went on, stealing the papers

IF A TWELVE-YEAR-OLD BOY MAKES A DOLLAR OR SO, WHO REALLY CARES?

became easier and easier. Matt seldom thought o
whether it was right or wrong. He simply took th
papers, delivered them, and collected the money

Matt had almost totally forgotten about how
wrong it was until that Monday afternoon. As he
pulled the five papers from the machine, the
strong hand of a policeman grabbed Matt by the
wrist. He knew he was in big trouble.

STEALING IS EASY

There are many places where we could steal
things and probably not get caught—at least at
first. What stops you from stealing?

1. You are frightened?
2. You want to obey God because you are a
   Christian?
3. Honesty is important?
4. Your parents would be disappointed in you?
5. Other?

WHAT STOPS YOU FROM STEALING?

WHICH OF THESE IS CROOKED?

1. Cheating on a test?
2. Taking your brother's or sister's clothes?
3. Keeping your parent's change?
4. Borrowing and not returning?
5. Taking a candy bar from a convenience store?

Explain your answers.

SCRIPTURE READING: Philippians 2:14, 15

PRAYER STARTER: *"Give me the desire to be honest even when I want to do wrong."*

About to Burst

Running across the backyard, Scott stopped to hide behind a tree. Quickly he shook the two-liter Coke bottle, holding his thumb tightly on the top. Trying not to make a sound, Scott waited for an unsuspecting victim.

Suddenly Laura raced from behind the garage, a two-liter bottle of Pepsi in her hand. Without warning, he aimed his bottle at the running girl and sprayed wet, sticky soft drink across her back.

Laura screamed and then stopped to retaliate. Unfortunately, her cola missed the agile Scott as he lunged to the right and dashed behind the garbage cans. Laughing uncontrollably, he watched the drenched girl scurry off to find a hiding place.

As Scott's laughter died down, he peered from behind a tree looking for another victim. Squinting his eyes, he looked intently at the figure moving in the bushes. Rapidly, he shook the bottle, building up enough pressure to shoot his next prey. He looked again at the rustling bushes.

"Swish!"

A sudden burst of liquid shot across the back of Scott's head and neck.

"AYAH!" He pivoted and sprayed at whoever was behind him. Too late, Scott saw Ann scamper away behind a hedge.

"I'll get you Ann Aspergren. I'll get you if it's the last thing I do!" Half smiling, Scott ran full speed after her.

> **RAPIDLY, HE SHOOK THE BOTTLE, BUILDING UP ENOUGH PRESSURE TO SHOOT HIS NEXT PREY.**

15

GOD IS ALWAYS THERE AND READY TO LISTEN. IT OFTEN HELPS TO BLOW OFF SOME STEAM WITH SOMEONE.

BEFORE THERE WERE BOTTLES

In Bible times liquids were often kept in animal skins. Sewn tightly together the skins could be used to store wine, milk, or water. If left with wine in them for too long, they could burst from age and from the pressure that built up inside.

FEEL LIKE BURSTING

Do you ever feel like there is too much pressure building up inside you? Have you ever felt like there is too much to do—too much homework, too many sports teams, too much pressure to get good grades? Have you ever felt like you were going to burst like a balloon or a wineskin?

When the pressure builds up, can you think of someone to talk to? Teachers, counselors, pastors, parents, and friends can be good people to share problems with. But best of all, God is always there and ready to listen. It often helps to blow off some steam with someone.

WHERE DO YOU FEEL PRESSURE?

1. At school?
2. At home?
3. On the paper route?
4. On the playground?
5. At church?

Explain what you mean.

SCRIPTURE READING: Job 32:19

PRAYER STARTER: *"Dear God, lead me to someone to talk to about the pressure."*

The Snapping Turtle

"Put that down." Mrs. Paladin's raspy voice cracked like a pistol. Each word was a sharp, brisk shot.

"She never lightens up," Luann said.

"Pity her poor husband," Nancy agreed in a whisper. "Can't you hear her saying, 'Take out the garbage. Be home on time. Take your feet off the coffee table'?"

Luann worked hard to hold back the laughter. Finally she had to take out a tissue and blow her nose to stop from cracking up altogether.

"Who's talking back there?" asked Mrs. Paladin, sounding like a radio with too much static.

"What does she look like?" Luann asked quietly.

"What do you mean?"

"Just look at her. The way she crouches down at her desk, barely looking over her book. She looks like a snapping turtle hiding in the grass," Luann explained.

Nancy worked desperately to choke back the laughter. Her lips locked tightly and her face reddened.

"People are her insects," Luann continued. "Anything that catches her attention makes her snap. She even sees things out of the corners of her eyes."

"Burt, I told you not to bring that glove to class," the teacher chirped. "Give it here. Give it here."

"I hope I don't get a temper like that one."

> **SHE LOOKS LIKE A SNAPPING TURTLE HIDING IN THE GRASS.**

Nancy turned the pages in her book."

"You mean you don't want to snap at everyone?" Luann kidded.

"Nah, it makes you look dumb."

Luann accidently dropped her pencil on the floor.

"Who did that? Who did that?" Mrs. Paladin squawked.

TELEVISION TURTLES

After watching television for a long time, some people seem to get quick-tempered and irritable. Have you ever noticed your friends or relatives get that way? Do you tend to get quick-tempered after watching too much television? Why?

WHEN DO YOU FEEL THE MOST IRRITABLE?

1. When you are sleepy?
2. When you are hungry?
3. When you are too busy?
4. When you feel picked on?
5. Other times?

CHILL OUT

If you want to stop snapping, you might:

1. Count to ten
2. Ask God for control
3. Watch others who are calm
4. Take a deep breath
5. Put others first

SCRIPTURE READING: Proverbs 14:17

PRAYER STARTER: *"Lord, help me not snap at others."*

Feeling Discouraged

Long ago there lived a prophet named Elijah. A cool dude, he served God well. God helped him perform miracles and Elijah was able to defeat the enemies of God.

One day, tired, exhausted, and discouraged, the prophet plopped himself under a small tree in the desert and gave up. He didn't want to try anymore. It's the same feeling as when you want to run away from home or drop out of school or quit the ball team.

Elijah was in the pits. He could barely hold his head up and he felt like life was stupid.

The prophet told God he wanted to die. He said something like, "Life stinks;" he felt like a loser and there was no point in going on. Then, too worn out to talk, Elijah fell asleep.

While sleeping, an angel nudged the prophet and told him to wake up and eat. He looked around and saw some fast food: a cake of bread still baking on hot coals and some water. Elijah ate and drank and immediately zonked out again.

Later the angel gave him another wake-up call and told Elijah to get up because it was time to get moving. He could only sit around and eat and sack out for so long. If he was going to feel better, he had to get up and get going.

It's easy to get discouraged and depressed. Most of us feel that way. Some of us get discouraged often and have trouble battling our feelings.

IT'S EASY TO GET DISCOURAGED AND DEPRESSED. MOST OF US FEEL THAT WAY.

THREE THINGS WORKED FOR ELIJAH WHEN HE WAS BLUE WITH DESPAIR.

1. He told someone how he felt.
2. He took a nap and got a bite to eat.
3. He then got up and got moving.

It takes a cool head to do something when we feel terrible. But Elijah came out of his discouragement by doing these three smart things (I Kings 19:1-9).

WHO, WHAT, WHEN, WHERE

Who do you talk to when you feel discouraged?

If you feel lousy, what do you do to help change your feelings?

WHEN ARE YOU MOST LIKELY TO FEEL DISCOURAGED?

1. In the morning?
2. In the afternoon?
3. In the evening?

WHERE ARE YOU MOST LIKELY TO FEEL DISCOURAGED?

1. At school?
2. At home?
3. On the playground?
4. At church?

SCRIPTURE READING: II Chronicles 20:17

PRAYER STARTER: *"Dear God, when I feel discouraged, help me do something about it."*

Calm Down

"It's getting a little choppy!" Ryan's dad called from the front of the boat. "Maybe you'll want to sit down."

Each time the dingy would bounce on the waves, Ryan would grab the side and steady himself.

"These winds come up every once in awhile," his dad explained as he pushed both oars into the water. "Nothing dangerous, but maybe you better hang on."

Ryan watched the darkening skies as he tried to tighten the strap on his life jacket. Waves lapped against the side of the boat making loud, smacking noises.

"We aren't that far from shore," his dad tried to reassure his son. "But we don't want to get soaked on our way in. Are you all right?"

"No problem." Ryan's voice sounded a little shaky. He held tightly to the side of the craft.

A light rain began to fall from the dark cloud that hovered overhead. Ryan was chilly and damp. He could feel the uneasiness in his stomach. His throat began to twitch.

"I hope this calms down soon." His father continued to talk, almost like he was nervous and didn't know exactly what to say. "Try breathing deeply. It might help calm your stomach down."

"Don't worry about me," Ryan said weakly.

The boat rocked over the waves. Up and down, up and down. Ryan settled down, his head resting deeply inside his shoulders like a turtle trying to hide in its shell.

Rocking, rocking. Bouncing, bouncing.

WHO MAKES YOU NERVOUS?

21

"You sure aren't saying much, son."

Quietly, the pale-faced boy threw up over the side.

GETTING UPSET

Who makes you nervous?

1. Brothers and sisters?
2. Unreasonable teachers?
3. Pushy coaches?
4. Something else?

CALM DOWN

What works best when you need to calm down?

1. A glass of milk?
2. Playing ball?
3. A nap?
4. Praying?
5. Talking to someone?

CALM PARENTS

When your parents get upset, what do they do to calm down?

1. Take a walk?
2. Watch television?
3. Sleep?
4. Read?
5. Pray?

A CALM PLACE

Where do you feel calm?

1. In your room?
2. At the park?
3. At a friend's house?
4. In the family room?
5. At school?

SCRIPTURE READING: Matthew 8:26

PRAYER STARTER: *"Lord, give me peace for both my body and my mind."*

Buried Treasure

The moonlight worried Joey as he moved from tree to tree in his backyard. He was afraid someone would see him, but that was the chance he took every Thursday night. Lifting his feet gently, Joey walked carefully across the fallen twigs and crisp pine cones scattered over the ground.

Clunk. His shovel hit a tree and Joey quietly grabbed the blade to stop it from vibrating. When the twelve year old reached the wooden fence, he placed the shovel on the ground and removed a large flat stone. Then he began to dig up his treasure.

No one knew of this secret part of Joey's life. Every day he saved one quarter from his lunch money (except on Friday when he spent it all.) On Thursday nights, he would bring his four quarters out and bury them where no one would find them.

Regularly for eight months, even in the summer, Joey saved four quarters and buried them beneath the slate stone. He never took time to count the money, but he figured there was about $33.00 in his savings. A few times he had forgotten to save the money, so it wasn't exactly eight months.

"Thud!" The shovel hit the top of the coffee can that he had carefully buried. Removing some more earth, Joey lifted the can and removed the plastic lid. He placed the can on the ground and began counting out quarters. "Thirteen, fourteen, fifteen, sixteen," Joey whispered to himself. "With the four

23

I have from this week, that makes twenty."

Placing twenty quarters in his pocket, he re-buried the coffee can. Joey covered the spot with the stone.

"This should help buy some soup for the homeless shelter," Joey whispered.

O T H E R S

1.

2.

3.

4.

THE MONEY CHECK

Make a list to see where your money goes.

How much money did you give to help others this week?

How much money did you spend on yourself this week?

WHO DO YOU LIKE TO HELP?

Who has your family helped with gifts, money, food, or work? If you could, who would you like to help?

OLD CLOTHES

Where do old clothes go when you are done with them? Are they handed down to younger brothers and sisters? Are they thrown away? Are they given to the Salvation Army or Goodwill? Does your church collect clothing and give it to families? Donating your old clothes to those who are in need can be a great opportunity to give to others.

YOURSELF

1.

2.

3.

4.

SCRIPTURE READING: Deuteronomy 15:7

PRAYER STARTER: *"Lord, give me a generous heart."*

Fit of Rage

Naaman thought he was a very important person. A commander in the army, he was used to telling others what to do. But if someone told Naaman what to do, he got angry and threw a fit.

Unfortunately the commander became sick with the dreaded disease of leprosy. There was no cure for leprosy in those days, but a young girl told him to go and see a prophet who lived in Samaria.

When Naaman finally found Elisha, the prophet told him how to get rid of his leprosy. He had to go to the River Jordan and wash himself seven times. No medicine, no surgery, no long recovery time in a hospital. Seven washings and Naaman would be well.

Instantly Naaman threw a fit. What was all this washing in the river about, he wanted to know. Why didn't the prophet merely wave his hands in the air and tell God to heal the commander? Besides, Naaman argued, aren't there better rivers than the Jordan, like the Abana and Pharpar? Get real.

NOBODY WAS GOING TO TELL HIM WHAT TO DO OR WHERE TO DO IT.

Even though he was a sick man and might die, Naaman wanted to have his own way. Nobody was going to tell him what to do or where to do it. The commander flew into a fit of rage and stomped off.

Fortunately Naaman's servants calmed him down. Eventually the stubborn military leader listened to reason and chilled out. When he returned to the river, Naaman washed himself seven times and his skin became as clean as a child's, exactly as the prophet had said.

Many of us don't like to be told what to do.

When someone tries, we go into a rage because we want our own way. Some of us probably refus to even take medicine because we can't stand to be bossed around (II Kings 5).

THE AGE OF FITS

In your opinion, when are children most likely to throw temper fits? When do they fuss and refuse to obey?

Ages:
1 2 3 4 5 6 7 8 9 10 11 12
Explain your answer.

STRAIGHTEN YOUR ROOM

If your parents tell you to straighten up your messy room, how do you react?
1. Smile and clean it up?
2. Sneak outside and play?
3. Get angry and hold your breath?
4. Close the door and pretend to clean?
5. Scream and fall down?

FIT THROWING

When you throw a fit, how do you act? Describe your motions.

SCRIPTURE READING: Ephesians 4:31

PRAYER STARTER: *"Dear Jesus, help me obey when I should instead of throwing fits of rage."*

Brotherly Love

"Did you get your Nintendo?" Lonnie asked anxiously. "Yes, I did," answered Tonya, his older sister. She turned on the TV and began to unwrap the package. "And I don't want you to touch it. Do you have that clear?" She pointed her finger directly at her ten year old brother.

"I'm not going to eat it, you know."

"You just might." Tonya slipped the cartridge in. "You've done weirder things than that. Like the time you tied a parachute to the cat and dropped it off the garage."

"Sniffles liked that little trip," Lonnie insisted.

"You're a nut case. Besides, this video game cost thirty bucks." The screen lit up with instructions.

"Mom and Dad paid for most of it."

"Only half, buddy. I had to cough up fifteen dollars out of my own pocket."

Saturn appeared on the screen complete with its rotating rings.

"Well, you could at least share it a little," Lonnie groused.

"And when did you share with me?"

"I left my science project in your room."

"Oh, thanks; a dead mouse in a box. What a guy." Tonya began to type out choices on the keyboard.

"Some big sister you turned out to be. You can't even share with your brother." Lonnie stood and began to leave the room.

SATURN APPEARED ON THE SCREEN COMPLETE WITH ITS ROTATING RINGS.

27

"Hey, I just got it; okay? Why don't you come back tomorrow and let me get used to it first?"

"Well, all right," Lonnie walked slowly away.

TONYA AND LONNIE

1. Is Lonnie being a pest or is he just normal?
2. If their parents paid for half of the cartridge, does half belong to Lonnie?
3. What do you think of Tonya's behavior?
4. If you had a new Nintendo video game, would you share it or what?

BROTHERS AND SISTERS

Brothers and sisters are usually:
1. Good at sharing?
2. Average at sharing?
3. Terrible at sharing?

Explain.

SHARING WITH CHRIST

Which of the following could you share with Christ?
1. Time?
2. Money?
3. Talents?

How could you share those items?

SCRIPTURE READING: I Timothy 6:18

PRAYER STARTER: *"Lord, I want to share just as You have shared."*

Company's Coming

"Come on up, Cody," his mother yelled. "Larry and Marcia are here." Cody recognized the names. They were children of family friends who came to visit every once in a while. Instead of running upstairs, Cody felt his body tense up and he kept playing with his video game. The basement was one of Cody's safe places, and talking to people wasn't one of his favorite things.

A few minutes later another call came rolling down the stairs.

"We're going out into the backyard. Come on, Cody, we've got some chips and stuff," his mother called out.

Cody didn't budge. He merely zapped a few more characters on the television screen.

Ten minutes later footsteps could be heard on their way to the basement. Cody tightened up but just a little. His mother slid onto the couch next to the twelve year old.

"You coming up?" she asked gently.

"I don't know," he barely grunted.

"Larry and Marcia are really anxious to see you. They don't know whether to come down or what to do," she explained.

"I guess I just like to be alone."

"I know what you mean. Sometimes I like to be alone too," his mother agreed.

"There's nothing wrong with that," he added.

CODY DIDN'T BUDGE. HE MERELY ZAPPED A FEW MORE CHARACTERS ON THE TELEVISION SCREEN.

"There sure isn't. But it isn't smart to be alone too much. People are important and these are really good people."

"Maybe I'm just shy," Cody wondered.

"A lot of us are shy. But sometimes we have to push ourselves extra hard to be with people," she said. "Otherwise we sink underground like earthworms. And even earthworms come up sometime."

"What kind of chips do you have?" Cody smiled.

THE TIMID THERMOMETER

How often do you act timid or shy?

5   4   3   2   1

(With 5 being very often.)

THE TIMID QUIZ

1. Do you enjoy acting shy?
2. Is it painful to be with people?
3. Would you like someone to help you feel comfortable with people?
4. Do you make yourself be with people?

FACT: Most of us think we are shy, but we reach out and meet people anyway. Most of us seem glad that we spend time with people.

SCRIPTURE READING: II Timothy 1:7

PRAYER STARTER: *"God, help me reach out to others even when I feel timid."*

Lighten Up

Arnold almost smiled the day his computer software arrived. He had saved for months to buy the master edition of the chess game. Already he had conquered the beginner's set and now needed a greater challenge.

After school Arnold would hurry home and go directly to the basement. At supper time his mother would call him only to hear "Oh, rats," in return.

Arnold hated being disturbed while playing his favorite sport. While his brother, sister, father and mother visited at the table, Arnold silently wolfed down his food.

His every thought seemed to center on pawns, knights, bishops, kings, and queens. "You must be having a good time with your new chess game." His father tried to draw him into the conversation. "Ummmmmmm," was all that Arnold would respond.

"Are you winning any games yet?" his mother passed the squash and peas.

"Some." Arnold pushed a piece of meat into his mouth and chewed intensely.

"Well, if I had gotten something that nice I know it would make me happy," his father added.

"Yeah, but it only turns you into a zombie," his sister chirped as she reached for the bread.

"It isn't easy beating this game," Arnold grumbled. "I'd like to see you try."

"Arnold, you don't know how to relax and enjoy life," his brother volunteered. "Even when you get something good, it only makes you tight."

ARNOLD HATED BEING DISTURBED WHILE PLAYING HIS FAVORITE SPORT.

31

"Yeah, Arnold," his sister added. "Enjoy the good times. Lighten up."

WHO ARE YOU?

Which of these names come closest to describing you? Maybe two or three would be true of you. Who do you want to become more like?

Sad Sam?
Gloomy Gus?
Silly Sarah?
Pleasant Paul?
Happy Harry?

WHO'S HAPPY?

What are some things that make you happy? How do you express your happiness? Do you hold your happiness inside? What makes your parents happy? How do they express their happiness?

SCRIPTURE READING: Ecclesiastes 7:14

PRAYER STARTER: *"Thank You, Lord, for giving me so many reasons to be happy."*

Now. . .
Who am I ?

The Case of the Cocky King

King Nebuchadnezzar had a long name. (His father, Nabopolasar, had a long name, too.) He ruled the country of Babylonia for many years.

The king had a bride named Amyitis who came from the mountainous area of Media. Since Babylon had no beautiful mountains, Nebuchadnezzar had some lovely hills and gardens built to make his wife happy. These Hanging Gardens were later called one of the Seven Wonders of the World.

His main city was called Babylon. It had huge colorful walls with special bricks. Pictures of lions and hunters and chariots were part of the brick work. Its walls were so thick, chariots could be raced on top of them.

Everyone agreed that Babylon was a great city in a fabulous nation. Tourists were amazed. Visiting kings rolled their eyes. The people who lived there stood up tall and felt good about what they had built.

King Nebuchadnezzar would strut around his palace and brag about what a great place he had built. His chest puffed up. His voice got loud. The king probably had a silly grin on his face. But King Nebuchadnezzar never took time to thank God for the great kingdom.

One night the king was walking on the roof of his palace and bragging about all he had done. While his lips were still moving, a voice interrupted from heaven. The voice told the king

EVERYONE AGREED THAT BABYLON WAS A GREAT CITY.

Babylon is a great city!

he would lose his authority over Babylon.

Immediately the king was taken out and put in a field to eat with the animals. He ate grass like a cow. His hair grew long like eagle feathers. The king's fingernails grew like bird claws. Every day dew soaked his back.

After a long time King Nebuchadnezzar looked up and praised God for all that God had done. After he gave God the credit for building Babylon, Nebuchadnezzar's staff members brought him back from the fields to the palace.

His attitude toward God had improved tremendously. The king knew that "those who walk in pride he is able to humble" (Daniel 4:28-37).

THREE KINDS OF PRIDE

One says: My dad and mom worked hard to make enough money to buy our new car. They don't have to thank anyone. Dad's tough, macho, and wears designer jeans. So there.

The second one says: My dad and mom work hard to make enough money to buy our new car. We thank God for giving them good health so they can go to work. We're grateful they can keep their jobs because many people have lost theirs.

The third one says: My mom and dad don't like to work. They sleep all day and hunt for worms at night. I don't know why God doesn't give us a car. Which kind of pride is the best?

SCRIPTURE READING: Proverbs 16:18

PRAYER STARTER: *"Keep me from thinking so much about myself that I forget to thank You, God."*

I'm a great guy!

Cold Oatmeal

Come on, Holly," her mother said impatiently. "Let's get that breakfast down. We've got things to do."

"Hmmm," was all Holly could manage to reply as she slumped at the table.

"Get with it," Mother demanded. "You laid around the house all day yesterday. Let's get some food down."

Holly didn't move. Showing almost no signs of life, her eyes remained sealed shut, and her lips were motionless.

"We talked about this last night. I told you not to watch television past midnight. We have to get the back fence painted this morning before it rains. Say something."

Unable to put her brain in gear, Holly couldn't quite get herself to join in the conversation. Her idea of a good day was to sleep until noon and then take a nap right after lunch. Eating breakfast at 9:00 a.m. on Saturday morning was far from her idea of fun.

"Holly Brenda Langston!" Her mother practically spit out each word. "Sometimes I think you're just lazy. Everybody else has to work around here while you lie around like Dracula."

Mrs. Langston wedged a spoon into Holly's fingers and propped her wrist up over her oatmeal dish. The daughter's limp body still refused to participate.

"That's it, lazy bones. I'm going to put these dishes in the sink and then you better be ready to paint that fence."

As noisily as possible Mrs. Langston dumped

EVERYBODY ELSE HAS TO WORK AROUND HERE WHILE YOU LIE AROUND LIKE DRACULA.

Z-Z-Z-Z-Z

the dishes into the empty sink and then turned in frustration to face her daughter again. Her eyes opened widely as she saw the twelve year old still sound asleep but now with her hand, wrist and shirt sleeve sinking slowly into the bowl of cold oatmeal.

TEN QUESTIONS

1. Would you call yourself lazy? Why?
2. How late do you sleep on Saturdays?
3. If something breaks in your bedroom, do you try to fix it?
4. Do you volunteer to help your parents? When was the last time?
5. When asked to do a job, do you make up excuses?
6. Are there socks on your bedroom floor? How long have they been there?
7. If you were in a footrace with a snail, who would win?
8. Who is lazier, you or your brother or sister?
9. If killer bees attack your house, are you likely to sleep through the attack?
10. If a bulldozer was about to crush your bed, would you roll over to get out of the way?

SCRIPTURE READING: Proverbs 26:15

PRAYER STARTER: *"Dear God, teach me how to relax, but not become lazy."*

Scared to Death

Smack! Justin slammed the ball against the brick wall. He scooped up the white ball in his glove as it bounced back toward him on the pavement.

"Nice pickup," Pastor Nelson said as he came close to the twelve year old.

"I said, nice pickup," he repeated.

"Oh, oh, yeah." Justin was spaced out.

"Man, are you thinking hard!" Pastor Nelson fielded the next ball with his bare hands.

"I guess," the boy responded flatly. "You know, with my grandfather dying and all. It's pretty spooky stuff."

"You're sure going to miss him." The pastor hurled the ball toward the wall. "You two did a lot of things together."

"I never thought much about death until now. It's scary. Just POOF and you're gone, like that. Sometimes I wonder what it's like to die."

"Most of us are afraid of death, at least some." Pastor Nelson missed the ball and walked slowly over to pick it up. "That's where my faith in Christ comes in. I'm still a little nervous about dying, but I lost the big fear."

Justin smashed the ball harder against the wall as he bit his bottom lip.

"Look, I've got an appointment at the homeless shelter right now. How about us getting together and talking about it tomorrow? I'll pick you up after school and we'll get a soda someplace."

JUST POOF AND YOU'RE GONE, LIKE THAT. SOMETIMES I WONDER WHAT IT'S LIKE TO DIE.

"Well, I don't know," Justin groaned.

"Sure you do. And you'll feel better after you talk about it. Meanwhile you better work on that backhand pickup." Pastor Nelson sent the ball speeding toward the wall.

FUNERAL HOMES

1. Have you been to the funeral of a close relative? Who's funeral was it?
2. How did you feel about the funeral?
3. How did you feel when you heard the person had died?
4. Have you known any children who have died?
5. Do you have any questions about death?

WHEN CHRISTIANS DIE, WILL THEY . . .

(pick one)

1. Come back as chipmunks?
2. Become ghosts?
3. Live in swamps?
4. Move to Mars?
5. Live with God forever?

SCRIPTURE READING: I John 4:15-18

PRAYER STARTER: *"Lord, help me not be afraid of death."*

Jonah Was Really Burned

Anger was written all over his face. Jonah's forehead was probably long and rigid. His eyes were sunk back. His jaw was tight.

The prophet had lived through a terrible storm, been swallowed by an ugly fish, and preached to the people of Nineveh. Surprisingly the people turned to God and God loved them. All of that left Jonah ticked.

Jonah puffed out his chest and walked outside the city of Nineveh. There he found a shady spot, sat down, and continued to sulk.

Evidently there wasn't enough shade, so God performed a miracle. He caused a vine to start growing. The vine rose up immediately and gave extra shade to Jonah. The prophet was tickled to get the additional shade.

The next morning God sent a worm to chew on the vine. Soon the vine got weak, shriveled up, and croaked. When the sun came up and the hot wind began to blow, sweat started to pour off Jonah's head. Beads of sweat ran down his nose. His shirt got soaked under the arms. Before long Jonah was so sick he wanted to throw up.

Jonah said, "I'm so hot, I want to die."

Suddenly God spoke to Jonah and asked him a question. "Do you have any right to be angry because the vine died?"

"Yes," said Jonah, "I'm so angry I could die."

"Big deal," God replied. "One little shade vine dried up and you are so upset you could die.

"BIG DEAL," GOD REPLIED. "ONE LITTLE SHADE VINE DRIED UP AND YOU ARE SO UPSET YOU COULD DIE . . ."

39

Imagine then how I feel about a city of 120,000 people who are lost without Me. You get rattled over vines, but I get rattled over people" (Jonah 4)

ANGER TEST

1. What makes you angry?
2. How many times a day do you get angry?
3. How long do you stay angry?
4. Do you quickly forgive people?
5. Do you get angry more often or less often than you used to?

NOT ALL BAD

Sometimes anger can be good. Jesus became angry several times that we know of. The problem with anger is:

1. We get angry too often.
2. We get angry over little things (like Jonah did).
3. We stay angry too long.

SCRIPTURE READING: James 1:19

PRAYER STARTER: *"Lord, help me put a lid on my anger so I don't blow up so quickly."*

Sandy Lost Her Cool

When Sandy arrived at the store it was already fifteen minutes before nine. She had tried to get her mother to drive faster, but her mother refused and told her daughter to calm down. After all, adding a porcelain doll to her collection was something that could always wait.

As soon as the engine was turned off, Sandy bolted for the mall and ran to the store. Her mother soon caught up.

"Oh, I don't see what I want," Sandy gasped. "They don't have any dolls with red dresses."

"Keep your cool, Sandy. Let's ask the clerk if they have any more."

"And what if they don't? We drove all the way over here and they are about to close. Do you mind if we go ahead of you?" Sandy tapped a lady on the shoulder.

"Sandy," her mother scoffed in disbelief, "let's not be rude."

"Ten minutes and they're closed," Sandy snapped back.

"Either you calm down or we're leaving," Mother said sternly.

Finally their turn came.

"I don't see any of the porcelain dolls with red dresses," Sandy glared at the clerk. "You had them last week."

"I'm sorry," the clerk said with a smile. "We're

> "I'M SORRY," THE CLERK SAID WITH A SMILE. "WE'RE OUT OF THEM."

out of them. But please leave me your name. More
will be in next week and I'd be happy to give you a
call."

"A call! A call! We drove all the way over here
and my mother was speeding."

"That's enough," her mother cut in. "You don't
need to call us. I'm not so sure Sandy is ready to
get that doll. Maybe she needs to grow up a little."

WHAT IF . . .

Your mother doesn't return your baseball glove?
Would you:

1. Hide her ski poles?
2. Put a raw egg in her boot?
3. Offer her $5.00 for the glove?
4. Nag her every ten minutes?
5. Ask her nicely to return it?

ACCORDING TO PROVERBS 16:32 A PATIENT MAN IS BETTER THAN:

1. A hog caller?
2. A sword swallower?
3. A chicken plucker?
4. A tight rope walker?
5. A warrior?

SCRIPTURE READING: Proverbs 14:29

PRAYER STARTER: *"Father, help me be
patient and not insist on my own way."*

A Party for David

Long ago, a Jewish leader named David went to war against a people called the Philistines. As commander of the army David did a great job defeating the enemy. Everyone liked David and were proud of what he had accomplished.

When he returned home, the Jewish people threw a gigantic party for the leader and his men. People were dancing in the streets. They sang happy songs and played instruments like tambourines, flutes, and guitars.

One of their most cheerful songs was:

"Saul has slain his thousands,
and David his tens of thousands."

The song mentioned King Saul because he was also one of their most famous heroes. What they meant was that Saul was a great champion and David was a champion also.

When King Saul heard the song, he didn't like it at all. The party was getting out of hand as far as he was concerned.

Saul and David had been good friends, but the victory party changed the king's entire attitude. From then on he was suspicious and mean and stopped walking close to God.

Because of jealousy Saul lost control of himself. Later he saw David playing the harp and the king threw a spear at his friend. When he missed, Saul threw a spear at him a second time.

Most people seem to get jealous sometimes and often it's because of a party. Either they

THE PARTY WAS GETTING OUT OF HAND AS FAR AS SAUL WAS CONCERNED.

weren't invited at all, someone else got more attention, or someone said the wrong thing.

Jealousy can change our personalities from kind and loving into nasty and ugly (I Samuel 18:6-16).

CAN YOU REMEMBER?

1. When was the last time you got really jealous?
2. What got you so upset?
3. Did you do anything dumb because you were jealous?

THE PARTY QUIZ

1. Who did David's army defeat?
2. What did they do at the party?
3. What did the special song say?
4. What was the king's name?
5. How often was the spear thrown?

WHAT MAKES YOU JEALOUS ABOUT SOMEONE ELSE?

1. Their clothes?
2. Their money?
3. Their looks?
4. Their intelligence?
5. Their hair?

When you start to become jealous of someone else, are you sometimes able to stop yourself and be happy with who you are?

SCRIPTURE READING: I Samuel 18:9

PRAYER STARTER: *"Thank You, Lord, for who I am."*

Losing a Friend

When Jesus heard that Lazarus was sick, He traveled to Bethany. But by the time He arrived, Lazarus had died. Naturally everyone was sad. Lazarus's two sisters, Mary and Martha, were there and their hearts were broken by the loss of their brother.

Jesus asked the relatives and friends where Lazarus was buried. In that area of the world many people were buried in tombs rather than placed in the ground. They told Jesus to follow them and they would show Him where the body had been placed.

As Jesus stood with the friends and relatives of Lazarus, His heart was moved at what He saw. The thought of going to the burial place made him terribly sad. Jesus was so sad that He began to cry.

WHEN WE FEEL SAD AND CHOKED UP, CRYING MAY BE THE BEST THING WE CAN DO.

Men and boys are often confused and embarrassed to cry. Sometimes women and girls don't know what to do either. There is nothing wrong with crying when tears need to flow. When we feel sad and choked up, crying may be the best thing we can do.

Fathers and mothers cry; football coaches and cheerleaders cry; bankers, lawyers, dentists, and even Jesus can cry. When we feel the need to shed some tears, that might be the perfect thing to do (John 11:1-37).

Funerals are almost always hard. The death of a Christian means that the person has left this life.

When someone we love dies, it's sad to have to be separated. That's why the funerals for grandparents are often tough. Even though we know we will see them again in heaven, it hurts to say good-bye.

ADULTS WHO CRY

What adults have you seen cry?
Did you understand why they were crying?
Have you seen adults on television cry?
Do you know why they were crying?
Sometimes people cry when they're really happy, but often it's because they're sad.

REASONS TO CRY

Would you be most likely to cry if:
1. Your pet died?
2. Your TV broke?
3. Your team lost?
4. Your parent was sick?
5. Your friend moved?

IF YOU . . .

lost some of your allowance, how would you feel?
were hit hard with a softball, how would you feel?
saw someone else cry, how would you feel?

Do you think God ever cries? Why do you think that?

SCRIPTURE READING: John 11:35

PRAYER STARTER: *"O Lord, help me to show my feelings when I need to."*

Hiding in the Attic

"Nick, are you up here?" his father called. "Nick!" He received no answer. Mr. Blanders walked past the bathroom and started down the hall.

"Nick."

At the end of the hall he could see the steps leading to the attic. His search took him up the stairs and soon he was in a large, dark room.

"Are you in here, Nick? Answer me."

He saw the faint figure of his son sitting motionlessly, half hidden by a few old storage boxes.

"We were beginning to worry, son. Everyone else has started eating. What's wrong?"

"It's nothing."

"Well, you don't very often hide behind boxes in the attic." Mr. Blanders sat down on a trunk near his son.

"You better go eat," Nick said solemnly.

"No hurry. Besides, it's meatloaf," his father said with a smile.

"I want to be alone," Nick declared.

"That's all right with me, but I don't think you are ever really alone."

"I am."

"If you want, I'll just leave you here alone with God."

"God already left," Nick said sadly.

"Just what time did He leave?"

"I mess up so much. I think God gave up on me

"I MESS UP SO MUCH. I THINK GOD GAVE UP ON ME A LONG TIME AGO."

a long time ago."

"That's how you feel."

"That's how it is," Nick insisted.

"Why would God leave you?"

"I just mess up too much. God must just give up on me," said Nick.

"That's one of the great things about God. Nothing, absolutely nothing, can ever separate us from the love of God. Love doesn't give up on people."

"I don't feel like God should love me," added Nick.

"There is more to it than feelings. You may not always feel like my son, but you always will be."

WHAT MAKES US FEEL SEPARATED FROM THE LOVE OF GOD?

1. A steel wall?
2. A trip to a cave?
3. An armored car?
4. Prison?
5. Nothing?

When do you feel like God is far away? Why do you feel that way? Feelings do not make it true. God is always with you.

GETTING DARK

When the room is dark, we can't see the wall. But the wall is there. If we feel separated from God, that doesn't mean God took a hike and left us alone.

SCRIPTURE READING: Romans 8:38, 39

PRAYER STARTER: *"Dear Jesus, thanks for always being around."*

I can't see you... Are you there?

He Lost His Head

BEING A PROPHET must be a hard job. When he says things that people don't like, the prophet can get into big trouble. John the Baptist was a prophet who lost his head because someone held a grudge against him.

A king named Herod married his brother's wife. When John the Baptist heard about this, he complained to the king that he should not steal another person's wife. Not sure what to do, King Herod had John thrown into prison.

The king's wife, Herodias, hated John because of the prophet's criticism, but she couldn't hurt the prophet. Holding a grudge, Herodias looked for some way to get rid of John.

On King Herod's birthday Herodias devised a plan. She had her daughter dance for the king and his dinner guests. The king liked the dance so much that he offered the dancer anything she wanted, up to half of his kingdom.

Herodias's daughter asked for John the Baptist's head on a platter. Too embarrassed to go back on his promise, King Herod had the executioner cut off John's head and deliver it on a platter.

Herodias kept a grudge against John. That grudge resulted in the death of someone who was serving God.

Jesus taught us to forgive people quickly; if we don't, we hold grudges and sometimes do dumb things. Getting even and hating people are feelings which usually cause trouble (Matthew 14:1-12).

HOLDING A GRUDGE, HERODIAS LOOKED FOR SOME WAY TO GET RID OF JOHN.

THE ROYAL QUIZ
1. What was the king's name?
2. Who did Herod marry?
3. Who did the dancing?
4. What did the king offer the dancer?
5. What does "holding a grudge" mean?

GETTING EVEN
Have you ever held a grudge and gotten even with someone? What was it like? Did you ever start to hold a grudge but decided to forgive the person instead?

BROTHERS AND SISTERS
Do you think brothers and sisters are good at forgiving and forgetting? Are they likely to stay angry and try to get even? Is there something you need to forgive your brother or sister for?

Aren't you glad . . . that God doesn't hold grudges against us?

SCRIPTURE READING: Mark 6:19

PRAYER STARTER: *"God, help me to let go and stop holding grudges.*

Is It True?

"This is the part I hate." Marti pushed a worm onto the metal hook. "Yuck!" She wiped her hand on her jeans.

"It's messy," her father chuckled. "But the fish sure do love them." He cast his line out and watched the hook sink into the water.

"What did you learn in Sunday school this morning?" he asked.

"Oh, it was that story about Jesus walking on the water." Marti cast her line out near the log floating in the lake.

"Pretty neat story, isn't it?" her father smiled.

"Well, I don't know," she said haltingly. "Sometimes I think it's a pretty tall tale. I mean, what if He was really walking on rocks or something. I mean, you never know what really happened."

"You aren't trying to tell me you have some doubts, are you?" He started turning his reel to move his line.

"Sometimes I do wonder. I guess that's pretty bad of me. I mean, to wonder about Bible stories and stuff."

"Nah, that isn't so weird. Most of us have questions sometimes. Doubt isn't bad. Lots of times our doubts make us become stronger believers."

"I don't doubt all the time. It's just sometimes I wonder about Jonah and the fish or Daniel and those lions. Stuff like that."

"There isn't anything wrong with asking questions. I think I've got something. Why not tell your teacher what you are thinking?"

> **DOUBT ISN'T BAD. LOTS OF TIMES OUR DOUBTS MAKE US BECOME STRONGER BELIEVERS.**

51

"But she would only laugh at me."

"Not Mrs. Adamson. She seems like the levelheaded type. I've got something for sure. Get me that net. Besides, Thomas in the Bible had doubts and Jesus didn't laugh at him. I've got it! I've got it!"

Marti broke into laughter as her father pulled in a large black boot.

WHO TO TALK TO

If you have doubts about your faith, who do you talk to?

1. Your teacher?
2. Your pastor?
3. Your parents?
4. Your friends?
5. Your dog, Hector?

PASSING DOUBTS

Most of us go through periods of doubts. Sometimes those periods last for a day, a week, or even a year or more. Most of us return to believe again. Don't let the doubts worry you. When deep doubts come, try to concentrate on what you do believe about Jesus Christ.

LOOK AT THOMAS

We call him Doubting Thomas because he refused to believe that Jesus was alive until he saw the wounds on Jesus. Christ didn't ridicule Thomas because he had doubts; instead He invited the disciple to touch His wounds. Read all about it in John 20:24-29.

SCRIPTURE READING: Jude 22

PRAYER STARTER: *"Lord, I believe; help me when I have doubts about You or Your Word."*

A Nervous Wreck

There were two sisters who lived in a village. Each had her own personality. One of them was calm and cool. She didn't shake up easily. The other sister was always busy. She had to be moving all the time and couldn't sit still.

The name of the calm sister was Mary. The hyper one was Martha.

One day Jesus came to see nervous Martha and cool Mary. Mary sat next to Jesus and listened quietly to the amazing things He had to say. She probably asked some questions and paid good attention.

On the other hand, Martha was a bundle of energy. While Jesus talked, Martha was up moving. She was probably busy cooking and rattling pans. Martha couldn't stay in one place. She kept grabbing cups and pouring drinks and hunting for napkins. You can picture her rearranging a piece of carpet, straightening curtains, and shifting the candles around. Martha was fidgety.

Martha was such a nervous wreck that she couldn't stand to see her sister, Mary, sitting so calmly. Finally she complained to Jesus.

"Is this fair?" she wanted to know. "How come Mary gets to sit around while I have so much to do? Make her get up and help me," she told Jesus.

But Jesus refused to get caught up in Martha's busyness. He sort of told her to chill out. He said this time Mary was acting smart. Martha was worried about too many things, and really needed

HOW COME MARY GETS TO SIT AROUND WHILE I HAVE SO MUCH TO DO?

to give it a rest.

Martha would have been better off if she could simply cool her engines a bit, and spend some quiet time with Jesus Christ (Luke 10:38-42).

FIDGETY

What kind of situations make you nervous?
1. Eating meals?
2. Being alone?
3. Meeting new people?
4. Watching TV?
5. Almost everything?

Why do those make you nervous?

CALMING DOWN

When you feel like you are too nervous (your engine is running too fast), what do you do to calm down?

READ   **PRAY**   **RUN**

NAP   **TALK**

Do you ever ask Jesus Christ to help calm you down? Do you ask Him to help you solve problems or help you take it easy?

ASSIGNMENT: Ask a friend what he or she does to help calm down.

SCRIPTURE READING: I Peter 5:7

PRAYER STARTER: *"Lord, help me so I won't worry about too many things."*

blah, blah, blah, blah, blah, Gab, gab, gab, gab, gab.. gab....

Grumble, Grumble

After Moses led the people of Israel through the Red Sea and out of Egypt, they had some hard times. After three days in the desert they were unable to find water and they started grumbling (Exodus 15:24).

The Lord gave the Israelites drinking water, but before long they were out of food. Again, they began to grumble. Why hadn't they stayed in Egypt, they muttered. They would rather have died in Egypt instead of starving in the desert, they complained (Exodus 16:2).

The Lord sent food to the unhappy Israelites. Plenty of meat and bread became available. But before too long the Israelites started grumbling again. This time they were griping because they didn't have water. Many of the Jews wished they had stayed in Egypt instead of following the Lord (Exodus 17:3).

Grumbling is like mumbling. When parents tell children to do their homework, the children often walk away grumbling in low, unhappy tones.

Do you often grumble because you don't have enough "stuff" like balls, bats, gloves, radios, tape recorders, or video games? After you get some of this "stuff," do you frequently grumble again because you want still more?

People who grumble seem to grumble no matter what happens. If they get something, they only grumble again because they want more.

GRUMBLING IS THE WAY WE COMPLAIN EVEN WHEN THINGS ARE GOING WELL FOR US.

Grumbling is the way we complain even when things are going well for us.

THE GRUMBLE QUIZ

1. What was the first thing the Israelites grumbled about?
2. God had delivered the Israelites out of what country?
3. What was the second thing they grumbled over?
4. Who was their Number One leader?
5. What was the third thing they grumbled about?

WHAT DO YOU THINK?

1. What is grumbling?
2. Do you have friends who never grumble?
3. When do you grumble (if you do)?
4. Is it ever fun to grumble?
5. Is it fun to listen to someone grumble all the time?

THE CURE FOR GRUMBLING?

Which of these things do you think would help stop you from grumbling?
1. A billion dollars?
2. A truckload of videos?
3. A thankful attitude?
4. A desire to help?
5. A desire to share?

SCRIPTURE READING: James 5:8, 9

PRAYER STARTER: *"Lord, give me a thankful heart."*

Stephanie's Neckline

"No, no, no," Mrs. Harrison told Stephanie, her eleven-year-old daughter. "Please don't wear that top to the picnic."

"What's wrong with this?" Stephanie whined.

"It's just not meant for a picnic. The neck's too loose for playing ball and horsing around. I'm surprised I let you buy that thing at all."

"That's dumb," Stephanie groaned. "You old people just have dirty minds."

"I'm not worried about my dirty mind. It's the boys' minds that concern me. Let's just get into something a little safer, and don't make a federal case out of it. Okay?"

Later at the picnic, Mrs. Harrison sat at a table with Mrs. Hilligas, her good friend.

"My Jessica is always trying to push the rules," said Mrs. Hilligas as she ate from her paper plate. "She sure doesn't like to be told what to do. She seems to have a rebellious streak lately."

"Stephanie's no different. I had the worst time getting her to change into that sweatshirt. You'd have thought I told her to jump off a bridge or something."

"They think we're a bunch of dinosaurs. You can't get them to turn their tapes down for anything." Mrs. Hilligas reached for a bag of chips.

"Now what's she doing?" Mrs. Harrison strained to see her daughter on the faraway ball diamond.

"She's taking off her sweatshirt," Mrs. Hilligas concluded.

YOU'D HAVE THOUGHT I TOLD HER TO JUMP OFF A BRIDGE OR SOMETHING.

"And she's got that top on with the goofy neckline," added Mrs. Harrison. "The girl's as stubborn as a mule. Stephanie! Stephanie!" she yelled. "You get over here!"

REBELLION

Rebelling is a lot like fighting. It's the attitude that you know more than your parents could ever know about what's best for you and your life.

Instead of rebelling, you might want to try talking peacefully with your parents about how you're feeling. Let them know what you would like to do and what you think is best. But listen to what they have to say too. Just talking about your problems may be enough to help you figure out what to do with your anger.

What do you and your parents argue over the most? Pick three.

1. CLOTHES   **4. HOMEWORK**
2. CASH   **5. MUSIC**
3. FRIENDS

Did your parents "rebel" against their parents? Ask them if they did.

ROUND AND SQUARE TABLES

Rebellion seems less serious in families that talk together. Does your family have special times when you sit at a table or on the floor and discuss your disagreements? Would you like to have discussions like that?

SCRIPTURE READING: Proverbs 17:11

PRAYER STARTER: *"Father, help our family to disagree without a full-blown fight."*

Finding a Tabloid

L ook what I found in Mrs. Carlisle's trash."
Mark joined Gerry on the picnic bench.
"They've got lots of cool stories." Gerry
looked eagerly over his friend's shoulders as Mark
began turning the pages of the rumpled tabloid.

"It has lots of good gossip," Mark said gleefully.
"It says the prince and princess are almost history.
She was probably just in it for the money."

"That's like the Weldons up the street. Their
marriage is on the rocks again," Gerry added.
"They'll split up before you know."

"Catch this! This guy cheated his company out
of $60,000 worth of duck feathers. Took them
home every day and sold them to a pillow maker.
What some people won't do."

"That's not so strange," Gerry explained. "Mr.
Stonehouse keeps adding lengths on his fence.
He's probably bringing that material home from
work. Boy, this is one sleazy magazine."

"Can you believe this picture?" Mark thrust the
tabloid toward Gerry. "This man has a dog that
can jump up and catch low-flying birds with its
teeth. Now I gotta see that."

"Man, that's something," Gerry agreed. "They
say Mrs. Nelson is training her dog to actually
attack children. She really gets ticked if you cut
across her lawn. Her dogs had better not attack
me. My parents would call a lawyer in a minute."

"How can they get away with publishing gossip
like this?" Mark wondered. "You'd think they
would have to be able to prove what they print."

ouch!

CATCH THIS! THIS GUY CHEATED HIS COMPANY OUT OF $60,000 WORTH OF DUCK FEATHERS.

59

"I think they don't really care." Gerry stood up to leave. "Some people just like to gossip and they don't care who they hurt."

WHAT IS GOSSIP?

To gossip is to tell stories that make a person look bad. The stories might be true or false. The reason we tell the story is to show an unfavorable side of that person.

If someone has holes in his socks and we tell everyone, that is gossip, even if they really do have holes in their socks. Anything said to hurt someone can be gossip.

WHO GOSSIPS?

1. Men?
2. Women?
3. Children?
4. All of the above?

GOSSIP HURTS

1. Have you ever gossiped about someone else?
2. Do you still remember that thing you told about that person?
3. Have you ever had gossip told about you?
4. How did it feel?
5. Does this experience make you want to gossip less about others?

GOOD GOSSIP?

There is no good gossip. A good story about someone is not gossip. A helpful story is not gossip. If a parent tells a child to stay away from a neighborhood because drugs are sold there, that information isn't gossip; that is helpful.

SCRIPTURE READING: Proverbs 18:8

PRAYER STARTER: *"Lord, help me control my tongue so I won't hurt others."*

The Death Sentence

The rich and powerful King Nebuchadnezzar of Babylon (modern Iraq) was bothered because of some dreams he was having. He was troubled by the dreams and wanted to know what they could mean.

Disturbed, the king called all the wise men in the land to come to the palace. Astrologers, magicians, and other people who claimed to have powers arrived and asked Nebuchadnezzar to tell them what the dream was. The king refused. He insisted they both describe the dreams with the interpretation or they would be chopped up into little meat patties.

The wise men did such a lousy job of explaining the dreams that Nebuchadnezzar kept his promise. He killed them.

Daniel was an intelligent man who had been forced to live in Babylon. When he heard about the executions he asked Arioch, the top guard, what had happened. Arioch described the problem.

Immediately Daniel went to the king. There Daniel learned that he also would have to interpret the dream. If not, he too would be made into bits the size of dog food.

Naturally Daniel was rattled. He told his friends about the king's threat and they began to pray. Though he was shook, Daniel took time to thank God. Despite all of his troubles Daniel knew God had been good to him.

THOUGH HE WAS SHAKEN, DANIEL TOOK TIME TO THANK GOD.

The young Jew thanked God for wisdom and power. He also thanked God ahead of time for explaining the dream, even before Daniel knew how to interpret the dream. He knew that God wouldn't let him down and he trusted God totally (Daniel 2:1-23).

THANK GOD—AHEAD OF TIME

Did you ever ask for something in prayer and thank God before the prayer was answered? It takes strong faith to thank God before you even ask Him.

PRAYING SCARED

Have you ever prayed while you were frightened? Why were you frightened? Was there sickness in the family? a tough test at school? family problems?

When you prayed, did you also thank God? Explain.

THANKFUL LIST

Take time to make a list. How many things do you thank God for? Swap lists with someone else.

SCRIPTURE READING: Colossians 3:15

PRAYER STARTER: *"Thank You for being a God who listens."*